# Zhou

Nick On

smith|doorstop

Published 2020 by
Smith|Doorstop Books
The Poetry Business
Campo House,
54 Campo Lane,
Sheffield S1 2EG

ISBN 978-1-912196-79-1
Typeset by Utter
Printed by People for Print, Sheffield

Smith|Doorstop books are a member of Inpress:
www.inpressbooks.co.uk.

Distributed by NBN International, Airport Business Centre,
10 Thornbury Road Plymouth PL6 7PP

The Poetry Business gratefully acknowledges the support of
Arts Council England.

Supported by
ARTS COUNCIL
ENGLAND

# Contents

*i.m.*
*Joe On (   –1949)*
*Barry On (1930–2018)*

# Zhou

One of the legendary Three Dynasties of ancient China which ruled from c. 1020–221 BCE and is traditionally divided into periods of the Western Zhou (to 771 BCE) and the Eastern Zhou.

The time of Confucius (c. 552–479 BCE), Zhuangzi and Laozi and the final form of the *Classic of Poetry* (c. 600 BCE).

The tenth most common surname in mainland China.

## Yellow Bird

the yellow bird stops
on Navigation Street
where my Chinese grandfather
dropped dead

his untranslated stomach said
'sickness is the seed of health'
so he bet on the *Yin-Yang*
and lost

he left his laundry
seven children
and a medal
from Chiang Kai-shek

the yellow bird stops
on the *paifang*
to the Chinese Quarter
where the bend of his little finger
beckons me in
to gather watercress

# Fragments of Zhou

*people came to him with letters*

Consider the unmarked square.

Select a character to bind
within its blank perfection.

Something simple to instruct the boy.

With brush hairs holding exact ink
make rapid strokes in running style
the tensioned gut of the drawn bow
the hook of the dragon's mouth
in the sharp curve of the *kou*
discharging without residue
into

        口 (mouth).

The boy is the hole in the mouth
the useless dragon of spring
who must learn the line –
the un-correctable line –
by the numbers and the lists.

Nine *Shi* of the dragon art:
hiding the tip, protecting the tail,
linking the scaly carapace,
emptying the grip, pillowing the wrist,
starting with force to move the mountain,
making strokes of bone, strokes of muscle,
uncoiling the breath of ink.

But the boy thought
           'Balls!
My testicles are *Shi*. These things you'd have me learn
are bricks to bang on doors with nothing now behind them.
There will be no chosen scholar on his couch,
belly full, reclining, writing eight-legged essays,
putting permanent names on mutable things
to the sound of beating gongs.

We will have to clear the middens of these mandarins,
grind their shit on ink-stones
and dip the tips of autumn pelts
in this most fragrant ink
and with our brush-pens dancing
list those who wear the *cangue*.

Our writing is destroyed in separate small pagodas
for euthanising characters
where Europeans see
the burning of books in little yellow kiosks.

I will learn just enough
to write a letter, to keep a ledger,
but not to lie in ink and cover facts of blood.

I have seen the suppurating docks
licked by Europe's clustered ships.'

*he spoke but little English*

Zhou made the nets –
wide-meshed for the big fish,
fine-meshed for the small.

I sit with Zhou in his small boat
and search the wide wide river.
Below the fish are plenty
and there's no need for heaven.

Some old fool on the bridge above
cups testicles to cross with crafty strides.
I laugh at him. The boatmen say:
'The river demon bites any dangling dick clean off –
to blow like a bamboo flute.'

I sit with Zhou in his small boat
and watch the wide wide sea.
Zhou casts his nets up to the sky
to save us from the storm.

Zhou hauls his boat on shore
to caulk it watertight
with oakum, grease and tar.

The children cry for food.
Zhou's nets have no fish.

If I put fish in Zhou's nets
will Zhou give me words?

He built a bamboo hut
and when it rotted in the rain
he built it once again.

Migrants came –
labourers and masons –
and cleared the fields
and dug the deep foundations
and built a vaulted monument
in the rich man's name
to stand ten thousand years.

He sat inside his bamboo hut
sheltered from the rain
and watched the migrants strain.

And when the migrants left
the empty vaults
echoed to no eternity.

He would shift his shack
and let the monument decay.

He built a bamboo hut
that rotted in the rain
so he could build it once again.

Look for me in Guangzhou
just where the River Pearl
inundates this elsewhere.

I am not home.

I am fishing in an autumn mist
        so thick it hides the dragon's head.
I am picking herbs in summer clouds
        so deep they hide the dragon's tail.

You will find a fishing boat
        stuck to the frozen shore
or the stones of a hunter's fire
        scarred upon the moor.

In the city they will say:
'We do not know this "Joe" –
there was a Chow from Fujian
who never went to school,
was servile to the richest men,
then a rebel, then a fool,
but he is dead and nothing now –
except a hungry ghost.'

You cannot fill the fourfold space with my date of birth.

But you may buy my portrait ready-made
and learn to paint the eyes of my blank face
without a brush.

We have barbeque, shark fin and côte de boeuf,
plain rice in the hovels, scraps beside the road,
and famine all across the fields.

Human flesh on the market bench.

Invective is an ancient art
an art of misdirection
point at the chicken
insult the dog.

The dog does not notice,
later its head turns
from white to grey to red to purple.

Old Fang's mouth was slit for speaking insults
to those that need not speak.
Speechless Fang mocked on in script:
      'Everyone has seven holes
      but All-full he had none
      they drilled a hole in him every day
      on the seventh day he died.'

I see no need to eat the faeces of my father.
I see no need to slice my flesh to feed my mother.

*he may have left a wife*

His queue was cut, her feet unbound.
He bought a Western suit.
She carved his melon. He broke hers.
She was frail and not so beautiful.
He threw knives to miss her head.
She did not know that she was dead.

*he came as a conjuror*

his capacious trunk contained
his conjuring equipment
his flowing robes of silk
his old opinions
locked

## Canto I

And so to the ship, with acrobats,
contortionists and

Zhou: the conjuror of the troupe,
the migrating magician
with his trunk of flowing robes,
his ribbons, devices and illusions –

> *like a bird in the clouds*
> *once gone, gone.*

> From the Pearl to the Mersey
> and every word unheard
> from the hole in the mouth.

> He left on a whim, a part of the process,
> intending to return;
> he ran from unfathomed concerns,
> meaning to found a dynasty.

A Sanyi merchant for a bunkmate,
a seller of silk, speaking only of silk,
despising Siyi Zhou.

Churning the sea to Suez,
steerage paid giving rights to land
and no passage to be worked
except through Suez
to dodge the duties.

Young Zhou on deck
shaking his hair loose at play
practising his act
entertaining the crew:

Xie and Zhang and 'Brilliant Chang'
who met in a river town barracoon
and shipped together to the depths of the ship
where the dragon's steam was hottest
the greaser, the stoker and the donkey-man
climate proof and highly frugal.

When there is no way out dreams are needed.

*Zhou dreamed he was a butterfly*
*and that butterfly was Zhou.*

Bi Cuide signed the coolie contract
and got twenty yuan on embarkation
and a dog-tag riveted on his wrist
and ten yuan monthly to his parents
and shipped to Canada by the Pacific route
and this to avoid the German ships
and was sealed in a train
and crossed a continent sealed in the stench of men
and dodged the Atlantic submarines
and came to France
and dug trenches
and repaired tanks
and lugged munitions
and learned in English – NO CHINESE
and wrote a letter home:

forget our quarrel the day I left
take care of our parents
when I return I will bring
money to support them
the rest of their days

and was set to clear the field of mines
and stepped on one.

*South of the Wall we fought*
*and fled westwards to the sea,*
*washed our weapons in the breakers*
*and lay be-shitted in the dunes*
*and the general would not stop.*

Who says the sea is wide?

*A single reed can cross it.*

## Canto II

The river town officials
wrote down what they heard
mistook family names for given names
and stamped the forms to make them true.

For 'Zhou' the pinyin patronym
                            write:
        Chou
        Chow
        Chew
        Chu
        Jhou
        Jou
        Jue
        Joe

And why should migrants be
fastidious with their names?
Let dynasties fall, as dynasties do,
into an amusement –
                        the disguise of a stateless conjuror.

The glyphomancer said:
    'Every name is fungible
    you will be marked as foreign
    you will not be marked Chinese.'

So he arrogated a name amidst
the antic and personate actors of the era
strutting with their jutting chins

and he was wary of definition
and saw that the world
longed for chaos.

The Exceptional Zhou became the ordinary Joe

    who

    lodged in the usual
    pushed his boats on-land.

## Dr. Wellington Koo

Dr Wellington Koo
at an official do
during World War Two
sat next to
the Alderman's wife.

Nothing was said
over soup and bread
so he nodded his head
and quietly read
his notes.

The Alderman's wife
gripped on her knife
as she sought a device
to connect with his life:
'You like-y soup-y?'

He gave a speech
in perfect English
which distinguished
at its finish
Anglo-Chinese friendship.

In the pause
of the applause
he turned with cause
and opened his jaws:
'You like-y speech-y?'

# Dispositions as My Father

Under the counter of the laundry
I am the boy reading Keats
The pot-bellied stove heats the sad irons
Smells of starch and drying cloth

I make a track in the words
My body moves without me
The counter's underside is rough
Its topside smoothed by soiled linen

The summit boiling clean
Makes mists of hanging steam
That rise through the spaces in-between
The floorboards of the bedrooms

The shirts and sheets of others
Washed, mangled, starched
Ironed, aired, folded
Smooth exchange of chits and coinage

My father handles the sad irons
Detachable collars need a strong wrist
The plump neck of Mr. Soo
Checking his packapoo

The Chinese seamen's hostel
Supplies of soap and starch
Slight men in baggy trousers, smoking
The sparrows' loud chatter: mah-jong, played fast

In a white silk gown
I am the alien boy
I keep my head down
Not to be seen

In the space between two rivers – atrocities
Against these he measures his homesickness
And saves me
The favourite son

# Gastrectomy Under Acupuncture

The pain in his belly was constant now
The body is to be endured
The cycle of opposites would provide a cure

> *gastrectomy under acupuncture*
> *six needles*
> *the patient: eyes open, rather anxious*

Lu Xun's father was denied a cure
By the time he knew he had died he was lying there dead
Someone said: 'Why should he die here?'

> *the man in blue has no gloves*
> *the stomach appears*
> *the patient's eyes are closed*

Where should a man die?
He wanted to taste his stomach
It hurt too much to eat

> *shrill noise of the translations*
> *his hand is not clenched*
> *the patient staring at us, bewildered*

Scatter the circle of soot

Dig up the bones to wash and store
in an earthenware jar
while the augur finds the resting place where the *qi* can flow
to soothe unhappy ghosts

# Copywriting

You shaved to Bach's *Badinerie*,
a pleasantry, heard either side
of the hard high buzz of your *Braun*
and the *pfuff pfuff* of your breath blown
through the razor's mesh to dust the sink
with stubble and burnt skin.

Your neck a size sixteen
yielding exact thumb space to collar
enough play to last the day.

Your shirtsleeves were half an inch too long
hence those mysterious armbands –
elastic metal coils that I would
twang and twist and think
was the working uniform of every grown-up man.

Your cuffs linked with things of wonder
wherein I thought my daddy was not poor
to go adorned in gold for lack of buttons.

Your scrubbed scents – *Badedas,*
*Metatone* and *Paco Rabanne* –
on your body and breath as you left for work.

Your daily drive of fifty miles to the Agency
in old cars, a succession of old cars
with throaty engines and things that moved
under heavy bonnets.

You said advertising was not illusion
but clarified the virtues of the things that would be sold.
Your clients were sellers of shoes and
agricultural feed.

One summer you brought us for the day.
We based ourselves in a vacant office
and found a stack of *Penthouse* in the desk
and were enchanted by commercial artists
who could make any mundane thing
come alive in lines from lovely felt-tip pens.

Your whole career was filling space with words
making every quarter-page and half-page
articulate with copy.

## *Taciturn*

At home you could be taciturn
while you waited for the circling chatter
to open to your wit or for your silence
to slowly spread across the room
and dampen our inanity.

On Saturdays you'd mow the lawn
your brow flecked with blown grass
as you quenched your thirst with barley water.

You kept things. Twelve electric razors.
An entire drawer of dead batteries from your hearing aids.

A week before you died you ordered
eight new business shirts with collars.

# Ghosts

### 1

*Pick a fern,* said Pound, *pick a fern.*
The poem must have energy.

Fiddlehead ferns fried in butter
to take the bitterness away.

But vetch is a starvation crop
to eat when the granaries of Zhou
are empty or else shut
against the gathering crowds.

Who would not eat the grains of Zhou?

Who says they'd rather eat the ferns
than taste of Zhou's corruption?

Only the ghosts, the in-between,
who sit silent in the snow.

*2*

How do you find the ordinary, individual man?

He is not in the books.
He is not found folded in the mass of migrants.
He is not seen in the stacks of starving peasants.
Of the nineteen students who were shot that day
he was not shot, nor was he a student.
He formed no movements and if he marched
he did so discreetly and was untouched by the purge that followed.
He left no manifestos and no short satiric essays.
He neither visibly oppressed nor stood against oppression.
Perhaps he ran, perhaps he hid, and in this he was successful.
Perhaps he stood still and gained respect from all the factions.
Perhaps he lived his life remotely, beyond tumult.

How do you find this extraordinary, individual man?

*3*

The little fingers of my father's father
bent inwards from the top joint
and so with his
and so with mine
and so with all our progeny.

A small genetic replication
neither defect nor aptitude
this clinodactyly
is a small and secret signature
a trace of ghosts
a linking ring
between bent fingers

binding continents
and strangers.

## 4

Silence is hard to obtain.

He would sit on a Sunday with all the windows shut
and all the streams of words and music dammed
but still hear the distant lawnmower
and every friction of the people's fuss
releasing noise.
So he would take a restless doze
or he would scowl and sulk
or he would smile and shrug
or he would laugh and say 'to hell with this'
and go and mow his own lawn
or put some Schubert on the gramophone.

For he was a man of every mood
who in later years went deaf.

## 5

Where is my father now
who let no harm come to me?

He has left abundant traces in the files
of an ordered life lived in an orderly time.

He has left his words and objects
his certificates, his passport
and his first pay-slip.
He has left his Shakespeare and his Mozart
his cupboard full of photographs
the paintings by his brother
and his father's family Buddha.

He has left a houseful of things
that he detached from long ago
and me
        and limping memory.

*6*

Small habits of my father are now in my muscles.

My scowl, my stretch, my nodding show of interest
are his, as is the very cadence of my walk
though not as yet decayed to that balletic shuffle
of the half-Chinese old man.
                                        He is in me now
and not in these objects that he used
however much they were moulded to his touch.

Even his Leica, through which for sixty years
he framed the things he found to view,
even his Leica is now a cold machine
the lens a number in a valuation.

But this gesture I am making now
this clench of my mouth that pulses in my cheek,
is him, as it was, in him, his father.

# Notes

The Cantonese word *Shi* means: power; influence; potential; momentum; tendency; trend; situation; conditions; outward appearance; sign; gesture; and the male genitals.

Italicised words in *Canto I* are adapted from poems by Li Po except 'a single reed can cross it' which is from the *Classic of Poetry LXI,* 'The River is Broad'.

**Glyphomancy** (*chaizi*) is a divination practice that involves breaking the characters that compose a person's name into parts in order to reveal hidden meanings about their inner nature or to tell their future.

**Dr. Wellington Koo** (1888-1985) was the Chinese ambassador to the Court of St. James from 1940 to 1946.

A **sad iron** was a heavy iron, suitable for stiff collars.

A **packapoo** was a lottery slip.

The words in italics in *Gastrectomy under Acupuncture* are quoted from Roland Barthes' description of a gastrectomy under acupuncture he witnessed in Shanghai in 1974. Reference is also made to two of Lu Xun's prose poems in *Wild Grass* – 'The Epitaph' and 'After Death'.

The first *Ghosts* poem refers to the *Classic of Poetry,* CLXVII in translations by Ezra Pound, Stephen Owen and Eileen Cheng. To 'refuse to eat the grains of Zhou' is to act with integrity as exemplified by Bo Yi and Shu Qi in the story told in Sima Qian's *Records of the Grand Historian*.

**Clinodactyly** is a minor congenital malformation from the Greek 'to bend' and 'digit'.